Stopping Bullets with a Thread

Stephanie Kwolek and Her Incredible Invention

Edwin Brit Wyckoff

Enslow Elementary
an imprint of
Enslow Publishers, Inc.
40 Industrial Road
Box 398
Berkeley Heights, NJ 07922
USA

http://www.enslow.com

Content Adviser
Nick Thomas, Ph.D.
Chemistry Professor
Auburn University at Montgomery, Alabama

Series Literacy Consultant
Allan A. De Fina, Ph.D.
Past President of the New Jersey Reading Association
Chairperson, Department of Literacy Education
New Jersey City University

Acknowledgment

The publisher thanks Stephanie Kwolek for her permission to publish her photographs in this book.

Enslow Elementary, an imprint of Enslow Publishers, Inc.

Enslow Elementary® is a registered trademark of Enslow Publishers, Inc.

Kevlar® is a registered trademark of E. I. du Pont de Nemours and Company.

Library of Congress Cataloging-in-Publication Data

Wyckoff, Edwin Brit.
    Stopping bullets with a thread : Stephanie Kwolek and her incredible invention / by Edwin Brit Wyckoff.
        p. cm. — (Genius at work! Great inventor biographies)
    Includes bibliographical references and index.
    ISBN-13: 978-0-7660-2850-0
    ISBN-10: 0-7660-2850-X
        1. Kwolek, Stephanie, 1923– —Juvenile literature. 2. Industrial chemists—United States—Biography—Juvenile literature. 3. Inventors—United States—Biography—Juvenile literature. 4. Ballistic fabrics—Juvenile literature.
    I. Title.
    TS1440.K96W93 2007
    677'.68—dc22
    [B]
                                                    2006034682

Printed in the United States of America

10 9 8 7 6 5 4 3 2 1

To Our Readers

We have done our best to make sure all Internet Addresses in this book were active and appropriate when we went to press. However, the author and the publisher have no control over and assume no liability for the material available on those Internet sites or on other Web sites they may link to. Any comments or suggestions can be sent by e-mail to comments@enslow.com or to the address on the back cover.

Every effort has been made to locate all copyright holders of material used in this book. If any errors or omissions have occurred, corrections will be made in future editions of this book.

Photo Credits: © 1999, Artville, LLC, p. 7 (map); Alfred Pasieka/Photo Researchers, Inc., pp. 3 (background), 18; Charles D. Winters/Photo Researchers, Inc., p. 17; Courtesy Daryl Wilson/Tulsa World, p. 24; Courtesy DuPont, pp. 1 (top left), 20, 22, 23; © iStockphoto.com/Micha Adamczyk, p. 27 (top right); Courtesy Smithsonian Institution, with permission from Stephanie Kwolek, pp. 6, 9, 11 (right); Courtesy Smithsonian Institution/Lemelson-MIT Program/Michael Branscom, pp. 1 (bottom right), 3 (top inset), 26; © 2007 Jupiterimages Corporation, pp. 4, 14 (bottom left), 27 (both center right); Lance Cpl. Erik Villagran/Marine Corps, p. 25; National Archives & Department of Defense, p. 13; Photographs used courtesy of Carnegie Mellon University Archives, p. 12 (both); © SCPhotos/Alamy, pp. 3 (bottom inset), 21; Shane Henderson, pp. 7 (inset), 8 (top); Shutterstock, pp. 8 (bottom), 10, 11 (left), 14 (right and top left), 16, 27 (bottom right); Susumu Nishinaga/Photo Researchers, Inc., p. 15; William J. Clinton Presidential Library, p. 28.

Cover Photos: Courtesy DuPont (front left inset has been color-enhanced)

Contents

This officer wears a vest like the one that saved Robert Miklich's life.

Chapter 1

The Deadliest Chase

A car went speeding through red light after red light on a highway in Pennsylvania. A state trooper's car followed so closely it seemed that both cars were attached. With his siren screaming, Trooper Robert Miklich stomped on the gas pedal, trying to get ahead of the driver he was chasing. Both cars skidded and darted through traffic. Finally the runaway car flew off the road and smashed into a bank of earth.

The driver threw open his door and ran into a field, trying to escape. Miklich ran after him. The suspect turned and shot Officer Miklich in his left shoulder. Blood poured from the policeman's shoulder. Another bullet hit him square in the chest, right over his heart. It was like being hit by a sledgehammer. But there was no blood. There was no hole in Miklich's bullet-resistant vest. His life had been saved by its threads. He handcuffed the man with the gun. It seemed as though Superman had landed in Pennsylvania. But this wasn't fiction. It was real life.

Stephanie, here three years old, spent much time around animals when she was young.

The genius who invented the threads that saved Miklich's life was a quiet woman who had at one time dreamed of becoming a doctor. Luckily for Miklich, she never did study medicine.

Stephanie Kwolek was born on July 31, 1923, in New Kensington, Pennsylvania. As a young

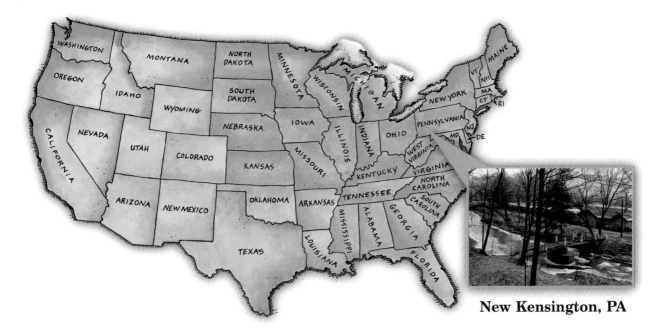

New Kensington, PA

Stephanie grew up in Pennsylvania.

girl she knew how to walk quietly in the woods. Even the tiniest frog would not jump away from her. A snake would glide by. Stephanie would not make a sound.

Stephanie's father, John, taught her to see and remember. Together, they watched spiders build webs. They found paw prints in muddy puddles.

Stephanie and her father enjoyed the outdoor world.

Their secret outdoor world was constantly changing. Stephanie liked to collect leaves and seeds, as well as skins the snakes shed each spring. She pressed her treasures between the pages of her scrapbooks.

When she was ten, her father died. He had given her the gift of patience stronger than steel. He had taught her to be a good observer, and to remember what she had seen and heard. Someday that would turn her into a famous scientist.

Chapter 2

Designing Fashions and Fibers

America was going through hard times during the 1930s. People called it the Great Depression. Factories closed down. Men lost their jobs. Stephanie's mother, Nellie, found it almost impossible to get a job. The family did not have much money. After a long search Nellie found a job. She started work with the aluminum company in town. Ten-year-old Stephanie took care of her brother, who was two years younger, after school.

Because of her mother's job, Stephanie had to take care of her younger brother every day after school.

Stephanie liked to sew dresses for her dolls. She wanted to be a fashion designer when she grew up.

Stephanie also spent time alone designing beautiful clothes. Her dresses looked as good as the pictures in fashion magazines. All through grade school she sewed clothing tiny enough to fit her dolls. Each stitch had to be perfect. Stephanie began to dream about becoming a famous dress designer. Her biggest dream was to show off her beautiful clothes on models in Paris, France. Her designs would cost a lot of money. Everybody would buy them.

High school was an exciting new world for Stephanie. The chemistry laboratory fascinated her. Glass beakers were filled with bright, colored liquids. She learned how to measure and mix chemicals very carefully. She heated them over a laboratory burner. The chemicals boiled and bubbled. Different things happened, and so she learned all about chemical reactions. She took careful notes. That made her think of her father. He had taught her to watch and remember what happened.

Stephanie enjoyed her high school chemistry classes.

Shifting from perfect sewing to precise chemistry experiments was a natural step for Stephanie. The good chemist in her became better

Stephanie attended the all-girls college at the Carnegie Institute of Technology.

and better. Her new dream was to become a doctor. Dreams like that cost money her family did not have. Stephanie decided to study chemistry at college. She planned to save money working as a chemist. Later on, she could pay for medical school. The Carnegie Institute of Technology in Pittsburgh, Pennsylvania, was a good place to study chemistry. She entered that college in 1942.

The country was fighting World War II. Millions of men went to war overseas. Companies were eager to hire women as chemists, engineers, and almost anything else. But when Stephanie Kwolek graduated in 1946, the war was over. Soldiers were coming home looking for jobs. Women began finding it hard to get work they had trained for.

Kwolek went to visit the DuPont company in Buffalo, New York. They did not offer her a job until she was able to convince them that she loved chemistry. They gave her a job searching for new ways to make thread and cloth out of chemicals. Kwolek moved to Buffalo. She would stay with DuPont for forty years, running thousands of experiments.

This woman helped build airplanes during World War II. After the war, it was harder for women to find jobs.

Challenging Nature

Nature has always made wonderful fibers such as cotton, wool, and silk. The fibers can be turned into thread that is woven into cloth. Cotton, which grows on plants, is made into sheets, towels, and all kinds of clothing. Wool is clipped from sheep. It is made

Natural fibers include cotton from the cotton plant, wool from sheep, and silk from silkworms.

into blankets and warm clothing. Silk worms spin out miles of silk fibers that make neckties, scarves, and expensive clothes people love.

Stephanie Kwolek and the other chemists at DuPont knew about man-made fibers like nylon. Nylon is made from chemicals found in coal, petroleum, and natural gas. Nobody had to plant fields of cotton. Nobody had to raise herds of sheep to gather wool. Instead, chemicals were

This close-up view of man-made fibers shows how they can be woven together.

mixed together to make fibers called synthetics. They were designed to be cheaper, stronger, and warmer than nature could make. Finding the right mixture of chemicals could take years and years of experiments.

Wells pump petroleum out of the earth.

Kwolek searched for new fibers by taking chemicals from petroleum, which comes from deep underground. Usually petroleum is made into gasoline for cars or turned into all kinds of plastics. Her job was to create the stiffest, strongest fibers ever made. They could be used to replace the steel built into the sides of automobile tires.

Her team of chemists made thousands of liquid fibers. Then they spun the liquid fibers into thread. Spinning means pushing the chemical fibers through tiny holes in a steel plate. Threads come out the other side. None of the experiments produced anything as stiff or as strong as steel.

Many chemists in the laboratory gave up on the project. But Kwolek's father had taught her patience. She kept on testing and studying. When the company built a more modern laboratory in the city of Wilmington, Delaware, Kwolek moved there in 1950.

Kwolek never gave up. She and her team made and tested more than one hundred thousand long chains of

Liquid fibers, like nylon, can be spun into thread.

FACT Polymers

Polymers are chains of chemicals attached to each other. They are made by nature and by scientists.

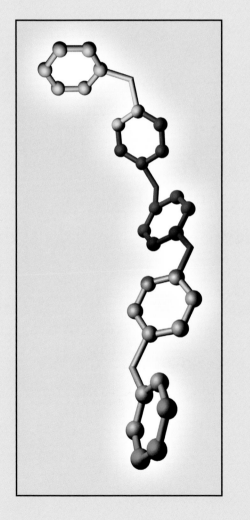

This is a computer drawing of a polymer chain.

chemicals called polymers (PAH lih murz). Her work went on for more than ten years. Most of the experiments produced clear liquids that flowed slowly like molasses. Some of them were spun into threads. Not one of the threads was stiff enough or strong enough to replace the steel.

Chapter 4

The Cloudy Outlook

"I made a discovery," Kwolek told a reporter. A batch of liquid chemicals looked cloudy and was as thin as water. She looked at it through a microscope. The parts of the chemical chains were straight sticks "like spaghetti lined up next to each other," she said. "Anyone who wasn't thinking would have thrown it out," she added. Kwolek did not throw it out. Her father had taught her to stop and think.

Kwolek sent a batch of this cloudy mixture to the spinning room. She wanted it spun into threads. "The guy in charge of spinning refused to spin the liquid," she remembers. He told her it would gum up his machines. Now Kwolek was a gentle person. But she never liked the word *no*. The man said *no* again and again. Kwolek said *please*. She said it nicely.

Kwolek used her microscope to see the spaghetti-like fibers in her batch of cloudy liquid.

She said it every day. "Either I wore him down or he felt sorry for me," she said, laughing, as she remembered the day the spinning began.

Kevlar thread has a golden color.

Something strange and different happened during the spinning. The links of the chains that looked like spaghetti lined up next to each other. Kwolek sent the thread to the testing department. The testers reported that it was nine times stiffer than any thread they had ever seen. The cloudy stuff was five times stronger than steel.

The United States Patent Office gave Kwolek and her boss, Paul Morgan, a patent for the fiber in

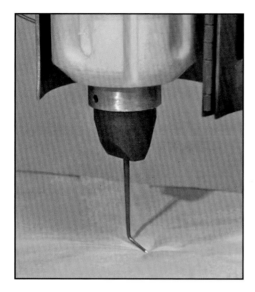

The material Kwolek discovered was so strong that needles testing it would bend rather than pierce through it.

1966. A patent is just a piece of paper, but it protects the inventors. It was legal proof that Kwolek and Morgan had invented the fiber that, later on, would be called Kevlar®.

There is still a giant step from tiny lab experiments to making huge batches of the same chemical in a factory. DuPont chemists worked five more years and spent 400 million dollars learning how to make cloth that could stop bullets. They struggled to manufacture rope strong enough to pull a train. In 1971, the first product made of Kevlar went on the market. Since then, more than two hundred products have depended on the unbelievable strength and stiffness of Stephanie Kwolek's invention.

Chapter 5

The Survivors' Club

Kevlar can be the difference between life and death. More than three thousand police and corrections officers are alive today because of body armor made

Threads of Kevlar can be woven into a fabric strong enough to stop bullets.

with Kwolek's Kevlar. It helped them survive many dangers, including being shot, stabbed, and dragged.

A policeman on a motorcycle in Oklahoma chased a car that was speeding at about ninety miles an hour. His siren blasted a warning. He flicked his headlight a dozen times and got so close he could see the driver's eyes in the car's rearview mirror.

All of a sudden the car became a weapon. The driver slammed on his brakes so hard the tires left 188 feet of black rubber marks on the road. Officer Ron Clark's cycle flipped on its side dragging him hundreds of feet along the highway. The car sped off leaving the officer for dead. He was scraped, bruised, and bleeding heavily, but very much alive. Without body armor made from Kevlar he would have been lost.

Officer Ron Clark's body armor made with Kevlar saved his life. His flipped motorcycle dragged him along U.S. Route 75 in Tulsa, Oklahoma.

Kevlar went to war in 1991. War is awful. It is not like a video game. Real bullets are shot at real soldiers. Even heavy steel armor may not save human lives. Since 1991 American and British soldiers have worn helmets made with Kevlar. Soldiers also wear body armor made with Kevlar to stop bullets and bombs.

"Not in a thousand years did I think the discovery of Kevlar would save thousands of lives," Stephanie Kwolek said. She was not thinking about war

In September 2006, Corporal Daniel Greenwald was shot in the head by a sniper in Iraq. Thanks to the Kevlar in his helmet, he escaped with only an inch-long cut in his forehead.

when she invented Kevlar. Her job was to think about stiffness and strength. Now there is a

Kwolek holds a model of the Kevlar polymer.

survivors' club of police officers. Some of them ask Kwolek to sign their precious vests.

Young Stephanie wanted to save lives as a doctor. Instead, she grew up and learned to save lives as a chemist. Kwolek spoke from her heart when she said, "I feel very humble. I feel very lucky. So many people work all their lives and they don't have a big break or make a discovery that's of benefit to other people."

Kwolek remembered her years of work. "I seem to see things other people did not see. If things don't work out, I struggle over them. You have to have an open mind," she recalled.

Kwolek retired to her home near the laboratory in Wilmington in 1986. The brilliant chemist never

Kevlar has been made into more than two hundred products. Here are a few examples:

* Bullet-resistant helmets for soldiers

* Body armor for police and soldiers

* Suspension cables for bridges

* Brake pads for cars

* Hiking and camping gear

* Sails and boats

* Skis, skateboards, and snowboards

* Outer shells for spacecraft

* Safety helmets for work and sports

* Safety linings for jet engines

* Radial automobile tires

* Rope strong enough to pull a train

Kwolek received the National Medal of Technology from President Bill Clinton in 1996.

forgot her love of designing and sewing. She bought herself a new sewing machine.

Her name is on seventeen patents and all kinds of honorary awards. Stephanie Kwolek still has that wonderful, wide-open mind. And, above all, she still doesn't like *no* for an answer.

Timeline

1923 Born July 31 in New Kensington, Pennsylvania.

1933 Father dies; mother goes to work for aluminum company.

1942 Enters chemistry program at Carnegie Institute of Technology in Pittsburgh, Pennsylvania.

1946 Graduates with bachelor's degree in chemistry; starts a job with DuPont in Buffalo, New York.

1950 Moves to Wilmington, Delaware, to work at DuPont's textile fibers laboratory.

1966 United States Patent Office grants patent for fibers later called Kevlar.

1971 Products made with Kevlar first sold.

1986 Retires from Dupont.

1994 National Inventor's Hall of Fame honors her work.

1996 Receives National Medal of Technology.

1999 Earns Lemelson-MIT Lifetime Achievement Award.

2003 Becomes 185th member of the National Women's Hall of Fame.

Words to Know

armor—Clothing to protect a person from swords, knives, bullets, or other injuries.

chemistry—The study of how materials, like fabrics, metals, and plastics, are made and how they react with other materials.

experiment—A test of something never tried before.

fiber—A very thin material, like a short bit of hair from a sheep. Fibers can be spun into thread.

Great Depression—A time starting in 1929 when many people in the United States became poor. They could not find jobs. The Great Depression continued all through the 1930s. Its effects were felt around the world.

molecule—The smallest part of something. Sugar, water, wood, and air are all made up of molecules.

polymer—A whole chain of the same molecule.

precise—Careful, perfect, absolutely exact.

retire—To stop working after having worked for many years.

sledgehammer—A hammer about three feet long with a heavy metal head. It is used to break up rocks.

survivor—Someone who lives through danger or hard times.

synthetics—Materials made by humans that copy materials made by nature.

Books

Casey, Susan. *Kids Inventing!: A Handbook for Young Inventors*. Hoboken, N.J.: John Wiley & Sons, Inc., 2005.

Thimmesh, Catherine. *Girls Think of Everything: Stories of Ingenious Inventions by Women*. Boston: Houghton Mifflin Co., 2002.

Internet Addresses

Chemical Achievers: Stephanie L. Kwolek
http://www.chemheritage.org/classroom/chemach/plastics/kwolek.html

Inventing Modern America: Insight—Stephanie Kwolek
http://web.mit.edu/invent/www/ima/kwolek_bio.html

Index

DATE DUE

J
B
KWO

Wyckoff, Edwin Brit
Stopping bullets with a thread

GILL MEMORIAL LIBRARY